Becoming Her"

I wasn't the pretty one–not back then,
Not in the mirror, not among friends.
My reflection whispered, not enough, In
a world too cold, and far too rough.

Raised in homes with borrowed names,
Where love was earned through quiet games.
Fostered, passed from hand to hand, Trying
to bloom in shifting sand.

Bruised by fists that wore false grace, And
lies that smiled from a lover's face.
I learned to bend, but not to break, To
carry more than hearts should take.

But time, she walks with wiser feet, And
now I stand, no longer beat.
I see the girl I used to be–
A flame that fought to still burn free.

At thirty-six, I touch the sky,
With every tear I let run dry.
The scars I bear, I do not hide— They're
proof I lived, I didn't die.

Not pretty? No. I am profound, A beauty
born from battlegrounds. Each wrinkle,
stretch mark, shadowed hue— A testament
of all I knew.

Now I love her–me–the child, the flame,
Who never asked to play this game.
But played it still, with quiet might,
And found in pain a spark of light.

So here I am, and here I stay, No
less than stars, no more to say. I
wasn't pretty, but now I see— I
was always more.
I was always me

Do you Know?

Do you know how it feels to be adopted?
No one really knows
What the pressure is like every day—
This is how it goes...
I wake up in the morning and stare into this face, I
want it to be a smile, but I feel disgrace.

A stranger in the mirror, skin I didn't choose, Love
feels like a gamble, and I always lose. Whispers in
my chest scream louder than a crowd, "Why
wasn't I enough?"—it echoes, long and loud.

Passed around like baggage, bruised but told to smile,
They hurt me with their silence, their rage, their denial. I
learned to shrink, to disappear, to swallow every scream,
To fake a life that looked okay, to bury every dream.

I hated who I was—my name, my skin, my past, I
thought if I were better, maybe love would last.
But years went by like shadows, and something deep inside,
Said maybe, just maybe, I deserve to survive.

I started picking pieces up, the ones they tried to break,
Spoke to younger me and said, "It's okay to ache." I
found my voice in therapy, my courage in a song,
Each tear a quiet battle showing I was strong.

Now I'm not fully healed, but I'm finding light, Learning
love was never meant to be a fight.
Yes, I was adopted, abused, and torn apart— But I'm
also brave, becoming, with a brand-new heart.

So do you know how it feels? You might never see— But
I'm writing my own story, and finally... it's about me.

To the Woman I Am"

There were days I looked in the mirror
and didn't know her name– Eyes too
tired, smile too quiet, heart too full of
shame.

I called it strength to stay silent,
called it grace to stay small, But
all I really wanted was to feel
anything at all.

I've been the girl with dreams too big,
the teen who dimmed her light, the
woman carrying worlds alone in the
silence of the night.

I loved others like lifelines–
gave them all I had to give, But
I forgot the simple truth:
I, too, deserve to live.

So now, I speak softly to myself
like a mother to her child, I
honor every broken piece that
walked me through the wild.

I am woman–still becoming,
with roots deep and wide. Not
perfect, but powerful, with
the moon on my side.

I honor the girl who held on,
the teen who made it through,
the mother who still rises with
strength she never knew.

Self-love may come in whispers,
not loud or dressed in gold, But in
choosing me each morning— that's
where the story's told.

So here's to the woman I'm learning to
be, in distance, in depth, in grace— I am
not a burden. I am a garden. And I bloom
in my own space.

Blood Didn't Build Me"

I have a brother, a sister— but
not in the way you'd think. We
share a name, a story's start, but
not the missing link.

No childhood memories, no late-night calls,
no arms when I would fall. Just silence
stretched through the years, a bond that
never grew at all.

Some say blood is everything, but what if
blood just watched you break? What if
the ones who should have stayed were the
first to walk away?

Adopted hands held pieces but
sometimes dropped them too.
Love came with conditions, and I
never quite felt true.

So I learned to raise my own heart—
to patch it with my tears, To mother
my own spirit through the loneliest
of years.

And slowly, I created something
stronger than they knew— A
family made of kindness, and
every scar I grew.

Friends who see me fully, love
without the chains, Laughter
in the living room that
washes out the pain.

No, I don't have roots that held me,
but I planted seeds instead. And
what I've grown is beautiful— not
broken, just rethread.

So when they ask about my family,
I smile and simply say, "I
built it from the ashes— and
I wouldn't change a day."

"July 25th, I Chose Light"

On July 25th, 2024,
I didn't just say "I do"—
I said yes to peace, to
joy, to a love so deeply
true.

I married a man who saw me—
not just the smile I wore, But
the storms I carried quietly, the
battles from before.

He held my heart with steady hands,
never asking me to hide, And when
my days grew heavy, he stayed right
by my side.

He didn't flinch at shadows, or the
weight my past had grown—
Instead, he lit a thousand stars
and called my soul his home.

But it wasn't just my heart he touched—
he loved my babies too,
Stepped in with strength and kindness in
ways only real men do.

He cheered their wins, he calmed their cries,
he showed up every day, Not as a
replacement— but in a love that chose to
stay.

The kind of love that softens pain,
and gives a second chance, That
teaches what forever means with
every passing glance.

So when I wear this ring, I wear more
than a vow, a date, a name—
I wear the proof that healing's real, and
love can rise from flame.

I married my light, my peace, my friend—
the one who helped me see, That love like
his, so whole, so true, was always meant
for me.

Still Standing in the Storm"
By a 36-Year-Old Black Woman in Philly

I wake up to sirens, same song, new
verse,
In a city where hope feels like both a gift and a curse. Where
corner store candles mark where young kings fell, And the
block cries louder than the church bell.

Karen on the line again — "He's suspicious," she said.
Translation: Black skin still equals threat or dread.
She clutches her pearls while dialing 9-1-1, And
another brother's life might come undone.

We shout Black Lives Matter, but the bullets still fly,
Sometimes from hands that look just like mine.
System taught us scarcity, bred despair,
Made us think we enemies cause ain't enough to share.

Trump made it cool to hate out loud, Built
walls, not bridges, to please his crowd.
Families torn, babies in cages cry, And
still some cheer while justice dies.

My womb ain't free in this so-called land,
Men in suits make laws with blood on their hands. Tell
me when and how I can bring life to the earth, But
vanish when it's time to value that birth.

I carry all this on tired feet,
Navigating cracked sidewalks and crooked police.
Yet still, I rise — Philly heart, black soul, Not
broken, just battered but wholly whole.

I wear my rage like a crown of fire, Turn
pain into poetry, grief into desire. To

build, to heal, to protect what's mine, In
this war-torn world, I still find time.

Time to mother, time to march,
Time to dream beneath the arch
Of a sky that ain't always kind, But
holds the prayers of my kind.

This is my truth, raw and unfiltered, A
life shaped by systems, yet never wilted.
Urban warrior, born of resistance,
Still breathing, still fighting — my very existence.

MAMA

Mama, at two I learned the taste of poison and fear.
You were there but never there, lost inside the needle's haze.
You whispered 'I hate you' while my small body begged for warmth.
Hands swinging, your love was fists crashing on my skin.

I remember the cold of the floor, the silence heavy as you dozed.
Hungry men came through, and you just let them hurt me.
You were too busy chasing ghosts to see the tears on my face,
too blind on your curse to protect the child at your feet.

I grew up surviving nightmares, with lullabies replaced by shame.
My backbone forged in hurt; my heart hardened in your absence.
Long nights I wished you'd wake to be the mother who might cradle me, but instead I held my own broken pieces,
stitching strength from pain.

In these city streets of Philly, I carry your shadow like poison in my veins,
With four little lives dancing at my hip.
I still call you Mama, damn it, because I'm dying to hear it back.
Instead I feel only the scar of your betrayal, my blood on fire in these veins.
I'm mother to four now, twice the woman you told me I'd never be.

I am the rage you left burning, an invincible flame in a black sky.
I am every bruise, every whispered 'Mama' that died on my lips.

I will not be gentle, I will not forget:
You are the ghost in my bones, The
villain of my story.
But I — I am the warrior you could not break.

I have four beats in my chest, four reasons to fight. I
cry when I lull them to sleep, thinking of your broken
lullabies.
But their bodies are warm under my arm; their dreams belong
only to me.
I learn love all over again, as fragile, and furious as a rebel's
heart.

So fuck your needles, fuck your apologies,
Fuck the silence you gave me.
I'm still here, breathing in spite of you.
Mother, I don't need your forgiveness; I
just need the truth: I survived.
And every tear, every scream, every step I take Is
proof of the woman you've failed to kill.

I am pain and I am power, Untamed
and unbowed.
I grow fierce for my girls and my boys, So
they will never know your damn neglect. I
am fire, cold coffee, gunshots in the dark,
And lullabies sung by my own voice.
I will carry you no more —
I reclaim the love you stole and keep my heart alive.

She Didn't Pick Me, She Bought Me"

You didn't choose me out of love— you
chose the check.
Signed the papers like I was property,
then locked me in a house that never
felt like home.

You called yourself "Mom," but your
love came with bruises, silent meals,
and eyes that looked right through me.
I was a dollar sign with skin, not a
daughter.

You dressed me up for show, smiled
in public like we were whole, but
behind closed doors you stripped
me of my voice, my worth, my
childhood.

Every word you spit cut
deeper than your hands.
"You're ungrateful,"
"You'll never be anything,"
"You should be thankful I took you in."
But what you took was my spirit, my
joy, my right to feel safe.

I screamed in silence, cried into
pillows, grew up learning love
meant pain and home was a war
zone. You fed me fear, then
punished me for flinching.

You never loved me.
And I've stopped pretending you did.
Because love doesn't bruise, doesn't

break, doesn't treat a child like a
burden with a price tag.

Now I carry your damage
like splinters in my bones—
but I also carry fire. The
kind that doesn't die, the
kind that rises and
reclaims.

I'm grown now.
Still healing, still scarred— but
stronger than you ever let me be.

And I'll never be you. My love
won't come with bruises, won't be
earned through pain. I know what
a mother should be— because I
survived what one should never
become.

They Took Mecca"

We used to ride horses, grip reins
like we ran this city, play fight on the
school bus, laugh 'til we couldn't
breathe, dance like tomorrow was
promised— but it wasn't.

Now I'm stuck here screaming, 'cause they took you
dirty. Right at your door, right in your chest, while your
heart broke watching' your mom take her last breath.
You didn't even make it out the house—
and I can't make peace with that.

We were just kids. Phone
calls after school, talkin'
about horses, talkin'
about dreams, never
about death.
Never about dying young.
But Philly doesn't care who you love—
bullets still fly the same.

They don't know you like I do— how
your laugh lit up rooms, how you
moved like joy in sneakers, how your
name was more than a name.
Mecca Likes-Harris.
That's my girl, my rider, my day one.
But now I'm just talking' to silence and
memories that don't answer back.
I'm mad.
Mad that I ain't get to say goodbye, mad that the
cops come after the damage is done, mad that
this city eats its children and calls it a Tuesday.

You were supposed to grow.

Graduate. Glow up.
Ride out.
Not bleed out.

They took you, but they didn't take your
name from me. Didn't take the way we
danced on that bus, the way we laughed so
hard we cried.
I keep that.
I spit that.
I live that.

You live through every verse,
every scream in my chest,
'cause you didn't go quiet and
I won't either.
You were love.
You were fire.
You were my friend.

Rest in rage, Mecca.
They didn't deserve you.
But I'll make sure they remember.

The Mirror Remembers"

You are not the bruises time forgot, Nor
the echoes of each battled thought. You
are more than scars that tried to stay,
You are here—you've made your way.

The road was cracked, your feet were bare,
Yet you rose from every snare. They told
you love must first be earned— But now
you know it must be learned.

Learned in silence, in the tears, In
facing down your darkest fears. In
every "no" that made you small,
You grew until you touched it all.

To love yourself is not a prize, It's not
the mirror's sweet disguise. It's
whispering, "I'm worth the fight,"
When no one else can see your light.

You hold the power to forgive The
past that taught you how to live.
Not perfect, no—but still complete,
With every wound that made you meet

The you that rises, raw and real, The
you that knows how deep you feel.
So love yourself through every part, The
broken bones, the beating heart.

Because your soul was never wrong— It's
always been your quiet song.
And loving you, despite the pain,
Is how you'll find your strength again.

To My Kids

I came up where the sun doesn't shine,
Where love got lost in the welfare line.
Mama did her best, but pain was loud,
And I learned young how to blend with the crowd.

I wore hand-me-down hurt and silence like chains, Walked
through storms, danced in the rain.
But you?
You gon' rise where I bent, bloom where I broke— Your
life ain't a struggle song, it's a victory note.

I built these walls from my broken past,
To keep you safe, to make peace last.
Ain't no ghosts in your bedtime prayer,
Ain't no screams in the midnight air.

You'll know love that don't leave, arms that stay,
A mama who'll fight every shadow away. You'll
eat when you're hungry, sleep without fear, And
know you got somebody always near.

I traded my trauma for bricks and plans,
Laid foundations with bloodied hands.
So you can walk where I had to crawl,
And never question if you're loved at all.

You all are my reason, my reset, my grace in the storm, Proof
that beauty still gets born.
I ain't just raising a girl or boy—I'm raising a queen, and Kings
Free from the nightmares that I've seen.

So run wild, baby—dream loud, shine bright,
I'll be your armor, your roots, your light.
You ain't gotta heal from what I survived,
'Cause I broke the curse to keep you alive

She Made Me Better"

I was lost in the smoke, heart running on fumes, Room
full of people but alone in my room.
Thought I knew life, thought I knew pain— But then
she came through like sunshine through rain.

My daughter—my mirror, my second chance,
The reason I finally learned how to dance.
Not in the club, but in life, in the grind, She
gave me peace I couldn't find.

Before her, I was chasing numb, Living
fast, trying not to come undone. But
holding her? Man, that hit different— My
soul got quiet, my spirit listened.

She ain't just my child, she my rebirth,
Taught me I was more than my hurt.
Now I move with purpose, walk with pride, 'Cause
I got a queen watching from my side.

I stopped running from what made me bleed,
Turned pain into power, 'cause she's what I
need. She made me softer, but stronger too— A
better version, someone true.

She the reason I pray more, love more, stay more, The
reason I got dreams I never had before.
My baby girl saved me—no cap, no lie— Now I
look in the mirror and hold my head high.

"The Life We Never Got to Live" ☽

You were just a boy of ten, A name
I loved, a could-have-been. Not
mine by blood, but in my heart, I
held a place, a hopeful start.

You didn't grow up by my side,
But in my dreams, you'd always ride
Along with us—your dad, your sis— A
life imagined, full of bliss.

I pictured birthdays, messy games,
You teaching her to spell her name.
Family dinners, weekend drives, The
gentle joy of shared lives.

But one day she just took you far, Like
someone stealing every star.
No warning given, no goodbye— Just
echoes now beneath the sky.

You've never met your sister's face,
But still, she asks about that place
Inside our home you might have filled—
A role that time has never stilled.

Your dad still holds you in his chest, The
son he loves, the boy he's missed.
He wonders who you've grown to be,
And if you ever think of "we."

So many bonds we never made, So
many plans that softly fade.
But still we hope, and still we pray
That life might bring you back one day.

We'll keep the porch light burning low,
In case one day, you choose to go
Back to the ones who always cared— Back
to the love that's always there.

Young Kings

Black boy, bold soul, born of the sun, A
crown not given—earned, one by one.
In shadows they try to dim your flame, But
strength runs deeper than name or fame.

You rise like rivers, fierce and wide, With
ancient rhythms in your stride. Each
heartbeat drums of kings before— Of
warriors, poets, truth at the core.

Your skin, a tapestry rich with pride, Tells
stories no chains could ever hide. Eyes
sharp with dreams, a gaze that sees
Beyond the pain, toward destinies.

You are not trouble, you are not threat—
You're brilliance this world won't forget. From
blocks to books, from beats to wings, You
shape the future—young black kings.

So hold your head, walk tall, be loud,
Your greatness doesn't need a crowd.
You are the promise, fierce and wise— A
sunrise burning through the lies.

The Edge and the Light

There's a silence deeper than sleep,
Where sorrow hides and shadows creep.
A whisper says, "You're all alone," But
lies sound loud when hope is gone.

You've walked through storms with broken feet, Felt
every failure, each defeat.
The world too heavy for your hands, No
one to speak, no one who understands.

Tears like oceans, hearts that ache, You
give and bend, but still you break. You
wonder if the pain will end,
If peace exists around the bend.

But pause—just one breath more to take,
A thread of dawn across the lake.
You are not weak for feeling lost, For
life, at times, demands a cost.

But hear this truth and let it stay:
The night is deep, but breaks for day. You've
lived through moments just like this— Where
light was nothing but a myth.

Still here you are. Still holding on.
A quiet fighter, dusk to dawn. You are
not burden, curse, or shame— You are
a soul still in the game.

And somewhere out there, someone cares— For
every soul, a hand is there.
Your stories not yet fully told.
Your future's wide, your heart is bold.

So if you're standing on the edge, Come
back, step down, release the ledge.
You are the storm, and you are the flame.
You are the reason, not the blame.

It's okay to cry, to break, to fall— But
please, my friend, don't end it all.
There's healing still, and skies to climb.
Hold on. You'll rise. Just give it time.

Guardians of the Light

They come to us with eyes so wide,
Hearts unscarred and full of pride.
Tiny hands that reach and trust— It's
up to us, protect them... we must.

Not just from bruises, breaks, and cries,
But from the wounds no one sees with eyes—
The whispered threats, the silent screams, The
shattered souls and stolen dreams.

We must shield them from the poison
lies, That say their worth is small in size.
From wandering hands, from cruel deceit, From
every danger their hearts might meet.

We are the wall, the voice, the stand, The
ones who hold their trembling hand. We
teach them "no" means just that—no,
That love is safe, and hurt must go.

We watch the signs, we listen close, We
speak the truth they need the most.
Because silence lets the darkness grow,
And pain ignored will overflow.

So be the fire that lights their way, The
strength that helps them find their say. Be
loud for them when they are small, Be
present, loving, through it all.

A child should never bear the weight Of
grown-up sins or twisted fate.
Their laughter is a sacred sound— We
must protect it, stand our ground.

For every child deserves to see
A world where they can just be free— To
grow in peace, to dream, to play... To
know they're safe every day.

So let's rise up, both fierce and true—
Because protecting kids... Starts with
me and you.

Still, I Rise, Little Girl

I was just a child, soft hands, small feet,
Trusting hearts in a house that should've been sweet.
But behind closed doors, the monsters came— Wearing
faces that knew my name.

Uncles, cousins, shadows in the night,
Turned my laughter into fright.
They stole my light before I knew
What pain was, or what a child should do.

My innocence—ripped, not lost, but torn,
Before I even knew why I was born.
A little girl with broken wings,
Held down by shame, unheard screams.

I carried silence like a stone,
Felt more alone than the word alone.
Smile for the world, cry when it's dark—
Each touch a scar, each look a mark.

But listen close—this isn't where I end.
This is the part where broken bends.
I found a voice beneath the pain, A
spark of sun inside the rain.

I bled, I wept, I cursed the sky, But
still I rose, I didn't die.
I turned the hurt into a seed,
Planted hope where they sowed greed.

Now I speak for the girl they tried to erase, The
one with power written on her face.
I took my story, raw and real, And
used it, sister, just to heal.

I am the storm, I am the flame, No
longer hiding in their shame. They
took so much, but not my soul— I
took it back. I made it whole.

So if you've known this pain, this fight, Know
you're not wrong, and you're not slight.
You are a warrior, forged in fire, Built
from ashes, climbing higher.

They tried to bury me in fear— But
look at me: I'm still here.
Still breathing, still glowing, still strong and wise.
Still loving, still growing—

Didn't Wanna Be Here

I was just a kid with a heavy heart,
Broken inside, torn apart.
Smiles fake, eyes gone dim, Drowning
slow, couldn't even swim.

Woke up like, why am I here?
Every thought soaked in fear. Hated
myself, my face, my name, Felt like
I was born in pain.

Mirror showed a ghost, not me, Trapped
in a skin I couldn't free. Thoughts got
loud, real loud at night, Wishing I could
just take flight.

Disappear, poof, never come back, Life
felt like one long heart attack.
Didn't want hugs, didn't want love,
Didn't want to hear about "God above."

Nah—where was He when I cried that deeply?
When I begged my soul just to fall asleep? When
I curled up tight in a cornered mind, Searching
for peace I'd never find?

But yo—
Somehow light cracked through that wall, Whispered,
"You're here? You ain't meant to fall." "You got scars,
but you got flames.
You ain't your past, you ain't their shame."

You're still breathing—that's the fight.
Even in the dark, you hold the light.
Don't let pain write your last page,
Don't let fear trap you in that cage.

You're not alone, I swear it's true— I've
been there and made it through.
So if you're stuck, just take my hand...
We'll rise together. We'll learn to stand.

'Cause life gets ugly, sharp, and wild, But
there's still hope in the hurt child.
And even when it doesn't feel fair— You
matter. You're needed. You're still here.

Cycle Breaker

They took me at three, too young to know
Why Mama let the poison grow. Bruises and
screams, cold nights, no peace— Just a child
praying for it all to cease.

Mama said she hated me, eyes so mean,
Not once the love I'd seen in dreams.
No lullabies, no warm embrace—
Just the sting of pain and a silent face.

My daddy died in '92,
AIDS took him, the rumors true. They
said he loved both him and her, But
left me lost in a world unsure.

And Grandpa—no, he wasn't right,
Came creeping in the dead of night. My
brother shielded me back then... But
later, he turned into him.

The ones who should've kept me safe
Taught me fear, and rage, and hate.
But somehow deep inside my soul, I
knew I'd never play their role.

I grew up fast, with broken parts, But
carried fire in my heart.
I swore my kids would never feel The
kind of scars that never heal.

No slammed doors, no hateful names,
No nights of guilt, no twisted games. I
built a world where love is loud,
Where trauma's buried, not allowed.
They sleep in peace, they rise in light,

They know their worth, they know what's right.
And every hug I give, each kiss— Is me
reclaiming what I missed.

I broke the curse, I fought, I bled, I
carry ghosts, but I'm not dead.
I'm still that girl they tried to break... But
I chose love for my children's sake.

So let them know when I am gone— I
was a warrior all along.
Born from pain, but raised by flame...
And I made sure they never felt the same.

Out of Place

I walk in rooms and feel unseen, Like
I'm a ghost caught in between.
A voice too deep, a heart too loud, But
still I shrink beneath the crowd.

They look; they judge but never know The
war I've fought just to show.
I smile, I laugh, I play the part, While
hiding cracks inside my heart.

As a kid, I learned to brace—
To mask the pain, to leave no trace.
Told I was nothing, made to believe Love
was something I'd never receive.

Hands that hurt, words like blades,
Nights I prayed the memory fades.
But trauma clings like second skin, A
storm I carry deep within.

Now grown, but still I roam,
Searching for a place called home. Not
a house, but peace, some grace— A
world where I'm not out of place.

Where I'm not "too much" or "hard to love,"
Where I don't have to rise above
The things I never should've known, The
battles I've survived alone.

Misunderstood? Yeah, that's me.
They see the mask, not what's underneath.
But I'm more than all my scars and fears, I'm
every cry that no one hears.

Still here, still trying to belong, Still
soft, still brave, still holding on.
And maybe I don’t fit their design...
But my soul is real, and it’s divine.

So if you feel the same, don’t bend—
Your story’s one the world will mend.
You’re not broken, you’re just rare— A
quiet light too true to bear.

The Grandma Who Chose Me

You weren't bound to me by blood or name, But
love like yours puts blood to shame.
When the rest turned cold, walked away,
You stayed—you never let me stray.

Even after the papers, after the split, You
proved that real love doesn't quit.
Not just a "step," not halfway there— You
gave me all your heart, your care.

Holidays came, you never missed, Each
card sealed with a handwritten kiss.
Birthdays bright, full of cheer, You
made me feel like I belonged here.

Tap shoes shining, lights on stage, You was
in the front row through every age.
Applause the loudest, smile so wide— You
held my pride right by your side.

You picked me up, no questions asked,
Turned lonely hours into memories that last.
Your house was peace, a sacred place, Where
I was met with love and grace.

You saw the pain they left behind, But
gave me safety, gave me time.
You didn't have to—yet you did, You
mothered the lost, the hurt little kid.

And still today, through joy and rain, Your
love's a balm, a gentle flame. You taught
me worth, you showed me how To love
myself, to rise somehow.
So here's to you, my chosen one,

Who loved me like a daughter, not a “some.”
You proved that family’s more than name— It’s
who shows up. And you always came.

The Weight I Carry”

Some days, I wake up tired, even though I
slept all night— like my soul’s been pulling
something heavy in a world that doesn’t
feel quite right.

I smile when I step outside, but
inside, it’s storm and shade—
trying to fake it ‘til I make it, but
this mask is starting to fade.

Anxiety taps on my shoulder, whispers
lies I try to ignore:
“You’re not enough. You’re falling
behind.
What are you even fighting for?”

Depression holds me like gravity,
dragging my spirit down slow— I
shower, eat, go through the motions,
but I’m barely letting it show.

I scroll past perfect pictures,
everyone shining and free, while
I’m drowning in quiet chaos
nobody else can see.

But I’m still here. Still breathing.
Even if it’s ragged and rough. Some
days surviving feels small, but
damn—it’s more than enough.

I light a candle, take a breath,
text a friend, say a prayer.
Little wins, tiny moments to
remind me someone cares.

I don't have all the answers, but I
know I'm not alone. This road is
cracked and messy— but it's still
a road I own.

So if you're fighting shadows too,
don't be ashamed to speak. It's
okay to cry, to stumble, and it's
brave as hell to be weak.

One step, then another— even if it's
slow and unsure. Healing ain't a
straight line, but every heartbeat
means you're pure.

You're not broken. You're becoming.
And even in the fight, you're whole.
You're the storm and the survivor. You're
the fire. You're the soul.

Philly Born, Philly Raised"

Born and raised where the bell doesn't
lie,
Philly skies, Broad Street pride—
Where the summers hit different, loud, and hot, and
every block got a story that don't get forgot.

We had water ice dripping down our chin,
cherry or mango—yeah, you know that win. Soft
pretzels in a paper bag, twisting' tight, salted
just right, every single bite.

Fire hydrants cracked open, water sprayed wide,
kids screaming, running, slipping in stride. We
didn't need no pool, nah, we had the street—
barefoot on hot concrete, Philly heat.

South Street strolls, music in the air, tie-dye shirts and incense everywhere. Sneakers in the window, murals on the wall, late-night cheesesteaks, answering the call.

The Gallery was the weekend vibe, posted up with friends, feelin' so alive. Grabbin' kicks, catchin' looks, chillin' in our zone, before they flipped it—yeah, we called it home.

Corner store hoagies, Faygo in hand,
spades in the park, dreams unplanned.
From North to South, West to the East,
Philly's in our blood, it doesn't ever cease.

We got grit, we got heart, we speak real fast, and we love you hard, with a love that'll last. From the El to the Linc, from the Roots to Meek,
Philly's got soul and a voice that speaks.
So here's to the city that raised me bold,
with stories in brick, in weathered gold.
No matter where I go, I carry the flame— Philly in my chest, always part of my name.

No Slouch" – In Memory of Elijah

They tried to stop the bond we grew, Said
love like mine wasn't meant for you. But
blood knows truth, and hearts don't lie—
You came to my door with pain in your eye.

Every day after school, you'd appear,
Backpack swinging, grinning ear to ear.
Shoes off, fridge open, jokes that'd fly—
We'd talk, we'd laugh, just you and I.

You found your peace where I found mine,
In quiet meals and borrowed time. You
told me secrets, deep and raw, Things
you'd never dare tell Ma.

I held your fears, your silent screams, The
shattered pieces of your dreams.
You said I was your calm, your space,
Where you didn't have to hide your face.

"I ain't no slouch," you'd always say,
Puffing your chest in your Elijah way.
And even now, I hear that phrase— Loud
and proud through memory's haze.

Then came that call—your voice, so low,
You said your boy was gone, laid low.
You were broken, torn apart, Grief
leaking straight from your heart.

That was the last time I'd hear your
tone— One hour later, and you were
gone.
Just like that, no last goodbye,

Just echoes of our lullabies.

The pain you left, it cuts so deep, Some
nights I can't even sleep.
I'd give up time, I'd give up breath, To
steal you back from silent death.

I wish we had just one more day To
laugh, to eat, to talk, to play. To remind
you once, as I always knew— You
weren't a slouch. You were true.

Now I carry your name in all I do, A bond
they couldn't break, not even you.
My cousin, my heart, my light, my pride— You
found your safe space, and it never died.

Dear Little Me”

Hey baby girl,
Yeah, you—the one with eyes too wise for a
world that never asked what you needed.
I see you.
Sitting on the edge of your own shadow,
trying to shrink into spaces that were
never built for your light.

You didn’t deserve that silence, that cold, heavy kind
that wrapped around your chest like chains with no
name. You thought love meant proving yourself,
pleasing people who never protected you,
apologizing just for breathing too loud.

But let me tell you something, and I mean
this with my whole soul— you were always
enough. Even when they tried to unbuild
you, when they fed you shame instead of
safety, you still grew.
Still smiled.
Still sang.
Still loved.
That’s God in you. That’s fire in your bones.

You survived nights no child should know, carried
secrets like bricks in your backpack,
trying to sit still in classrooms while
your spirit screamed.
You looked for safety in places that failed you, but
still—you kept searching.
You never gave up. You never stopped
hoping that someone might see you,
hold you, choose you.

I wish I could scoop you up in all your little pieces, wrap
you in warmth that doesn't ask anything in return.
I wish I could whisper to you,
"You don't have to be strong right now.
You can cry. You can break.
I'm here."
Because I am now.
I got you.

I'm the woman you became— the
one who took your pain and built
something holy with it. I held your
broken, stitched it into poetry and
prayers, and now I carry you
proudly like a crown, not a
burden.

You made it.
We made it.
Every bruise became a map, every
tear became a testimony.
They didn't win.
You're not forgotten.
You're not lost.
You are loved.

So rest now, baby girl.
Lay your little head on my shoulder.
You don't have to fight anymore. I've
got us now.

Built From Broken"

I was not born from ease or grace, But
from the ashes of a shattered place.
Where silence screamed and love ran dry,
Where every breath felt like goodbye.

They thought I'd crumble—thought I'd fade,
Under the weight of wounds they made. But
even pain, when pressed by fire, Can mold a
soul that won't retire.

I was built from broken—brick by scar,
Each fracture lit like a falling star.
The nights I cried, the days I bled, Were
stones I stacked to lift my head.

Tragedy knocked, it came to feast,
Dressed in grief, disguised as peace. But
I rose each time it touched my door,
With fists of faith and something more.

The storms that came to wash me out
Just taught me what I'm truly about.
They sharpened edges once too soft, Gave
me a voice that carries aloft.

I found strength in places dark,
Turned every bruise into a mark—
A map of where I've had to go To
find the parts they'll never know.

I am the fire that didn't die, The
buried root that reached the sky.
I am the story, not the scar— Not
what they did, but who you are.

So if you ask how I survived, Know
this: I didn't just stay alive.
I rose, I burned, I bloomed, I grew— Built
from broken... but built brand new.

Unapologetically Black, Unbreakable Woman

They look at me like I'm body
before I'm being— hips before
heart, lips before voice, ass
before ambition.

They unzip me with their eyes
before they even ask my name. A
Black woman ain't ever safe—
not on streets, not in schools,
not in her own damn skin.

We carry the weight of a
thousand wounds hidden
beneath smiles they
mistake for strength.
But survival ain't consent.
And resilience ain't peace.

They told me I was too loud, too
angry, too bold— but stayed silent
when I was touched without asking,
called "exotic," like I'm some damn
fruit meant to be tasted then spit
out.

They sexualized me before I
could spell the word. Eleven
years old, already grown in
their eyes. I learned shame
before I knew desire.

And let's talk about color.
Light skin?
She's "pretty for a Black girl." Dark
skin?

She's "strong,"
"intimidating,"
"masculine." They romanticize the
light, but demonize the deep brown
beauty
like it's too much for
their narrow sight.

I watched my sisters bleach their brilliance,
buy wigs to mimic proximity to "perfect,"
erase themselves to be seen, then hated
themselves when they still weren't enough.

But we are enough.
Goddamn, we are more than enough.
We are rage and softness, fire and
calm, we are the whole ocean— not
just the waves you ride.

We are the lullaby and the war cry.
The mother of civilization and the
mourning child. We are poetry in
skin, thick with stories that the
world has tried to silence with
every whip, word, and wound.

We don't always heal.
Sometimes we just learn how
to carry the pain better. How
to fake a smile quicker.
How to laugh without joy
because it's safer than screaming.
We get up, yes— but some days,
just barely.

Still, we show up. Not because we're
unbreakable, but because no one else will

show up for us. This world owes us softness—and until it gives it, we'll keep holding each other up with trembling hands, and tired hearts, whispering, "You're still here. That's enough."

All Black is beautiful. Not
the kind they sell, but the
kind that survives.
The kind that doesn't need your approval
to be divine.

Philly Psalms

He ain't hard, he's
just tired.
Tired of waking up to sirens and falling
asleep to gunshots like lullabies sung in
bass. Tired of being told to "man up"
when he's still just a boy learning how to
carry grief like groceries home from the
corner store.

In Philly, dreams don't come wrapped in college
brochures. They come in ounces, in corners, in
whispers about "quick flips" and fast money that
never sticks around long enough to feed a hungry
house.

He's 17, already a
provider, already a
protector, already a
target.
No dad.
Just mama crying behind a closed door
while the lights flicker and the fridge
hums like it's praying too.

It's either clock in or clock out—
Wawa shifts at 6AM, or running
packs with his cousin who
already got one foot in a jail cell
or a grave.

You think it's easy
when the job don't pay but the
plug does? When the rent's late
but your little sister's belly ain't?
When the world don't see you

unless you're in handcuffs or
headlines?

This ain't about choices.
This is about chances. And
most of them ain't given— just
taken.

But he's strong.
Not the kind that flexes in the mirror,
the kind that walks past temptation
with cracked shoes and tired legs.
The kind that stays in school even
when the streets offer faster
diplomas written in chalk outlines.

He writes his name in
notebooks, not mugshots.
And some days, that's the
only win he gets.

Black boys in Philly grow up with
their backs to the wall and their
hands in the air— not to surrender,
but to reach for something better.
Basketball dreams, beats in their
notebook, the girl next door who
said
he's more than the block.

But the block don't forget.
And survival here ain't
holy or heroic— it's ugly,
grimy, every day waking
up just trying not to die.

Still, he loves.

Still, he laughs. Still,
he lives with the heart
of a king in a city that
treats him like a pawn.

They don't write poems for boys like him.
But they should.

Because every breath he takes is
a rebellion.
Every choice to stay clean,
to stay soft, to stay sane is
a miracle in a war zone.

So this one's for him.
The Black man surviving in silence.
The teen with too many weights on his shoulders.
The boy with bulletproof hope and bare hands.

You are seen.
You are sacred.
You are still here.

And that's not just survival. That's
strength.

Perfect Anyway

I met you in a world full of noise, but
somehow, you were the quiet I didn't
know I needed. No fireworks, just peace.
No masks, just truth.
You didn't sweep me off my feet— you
helped me stand.

You're not perfect, but
you're perfect for me.
And that's a different kind of magic.

The way your hands don't fix me—
but hold me, soft and steady, even
when I'm unraveling. The way you
see through my silence, and love me
louder anyway. Like every scar I
tried to hide is still worth kissing.

We don't get it right all the time.
We disagree, we stumble, we've
seen the mess in each other.
But you never ran.
You stayed.
And I stayed too.

That's love, isn't it? Not
just the sunshine days, but
the storms—
and still choosing each other every
damn time.

You are my calm.
My chaos, too, sometimes— but
the kind I'd get lost in forever.
You're the safe space I prayed for

before I even knew what I
needed.

You make me better, not by changing
me, but by reminding me who I am
when the world tries to make me forget.

And I hope I do the same for you— be
the place you come back to, the peace
inside your fire, the warmth when the
world turns cold.

We are flawed. But together, we
are a masterpiece in progress— a
love story still being written, in all
its messy, beautiful truth.

And if this is forever, even with all the
bumps and bruises— then baby,
I'm already home.

2Faced (Torn Between Evil and Good)

You stand in the mirror, jaw tight, eyes
wild ain't no peace in the reflection,
just a war you been fighting since
child.

One half wear a mask, the
other one don't care to hide
and both of them tired, both of
them cried.

He walk with shadows in his chest,
a grin that cut deep, he the version
of you that don't lose no sleep.
Whispers in your ear:
"End it. Why keep tryna pretend?
This world cold.
Nobody coming in the end."

He remember every time they said you worthless,
every time you reached out and got silence. He
keep a tally of the nights you didn't eat, the days
you stared at traffic, thinkin' how easy it'd be to
just step off the concrete.

He say:
"It don't matter. You don't matter.
That smile they love? That's fake chatter.
Let go.
You done enough.
Ain't nobody gonna miss what they never really touched."

But then her
voice, low
like a
lullaby

soaked in
tears, the
kind that
break your
heart
'cause it sounds too soft for this world's spears.

She say:
"I see you.
Even when you try to disappear.
Even when your laugh's a lie and
your joy feels rented, not real."

She don't yell—she just sit beside the
pain, don't try to fix it, just holds your
name like it's still worth something.

She reminds you of that time you
wrote a poem and didn't hate it. Of
the kid you made smile when you
had nothin' left to give. Of the way
your heart still beats despite how
many times you begged it not to.

You the one caught in
between not wanting to
live and too scared to die
you shake. Not from
weakness, but from
choosing to stay.

You say:
"I'm tired."
She nods.
You whisper: "I don't wanna go, but
I don't know how to stay either."
And she replies:

“Then stay for now.
Just now.
Breathe.
That’s enough.”

The boy in the mirror still watches, arms crossed, eyes cold, daring you to fall again, like he knows the taste of rock bottom too well. But this time, you don’t blink. You don’t break.

You reach for her— not with hands, but
with hope. A trembling kind, the kind
that says, “I don’t believe in tomorrow,
but maybe... I’ll make it through tonight.”

And that’s enough.
Not healing yet.
Not whole.
But breathing.
Still cracked, still bleeding, but
alive.

You don’t need a miracle.
You just need a moment.
And in this one, you
choose life— not because
it’s painless,
but because somewhere deep beneath all the noise,
you still want to see what light feels like when it’s
yours.

You’re still here.
And that... that means
everything

What These Girls Want from a Man

(A Girls Reply to DMX)

What we want?
We want real.
Not just talk, but somethin' we can feel.
We tired of the flex, the front, the fake, Wanna
know: can you hold it down or just take?

She want love, but not that
half-ass kinda care. Not the
"you up?" at 2am with hands in
her hair. She want truth,
not just pillow talk and
games, Not a man with 20
faces and none sayin' her
name.

She want space to be loud
and soft at the same time.
Wanna cry on your chest
and still feel fine.
She want to heal with you,
not be the one always fixin'.
She a queen, not a rehab,
stop gettin' that twisted.

She want consistency— not
just calls when you bored.
Not the "you my girl" and the
next day you ignore.
She want someone who ain't scared to grow,
Who can say "I'm wrong," and mean it, bro.

She want laughs,
deep talks, long rides,

Someone who don't
dip when she show
her darker sides. She
want her edges
kissed, her goals
supported, Wanna
know her soul
ain't just bein' exploited.

Yeah, she want nails
done, but she pay for her
own. Wanna build an
empire, not beg for a
throne. She want sex,
sure– but not if love ain't
there. She tired of passion
that leaves her bare.

She want you to call her out
without breakin' her down, Want a
man who can lead, but still hand
over the crown. She want freedom,
not control disguised as care,
Wanna be chosen every day, not
just when it's convenient there.

She want loyalty, not just the
word in your bio. Not "my girl
bad" but you slidin' on the sly
though. She want family, maybe
kids, maybe peace–
But only if love's real
and the stress can cease.

So what these girls want from a n***a? It
ain't no mystery.
Just honesty, effort,

and a lil' emotional literacy. Be the safe space, not the storm she gotta survive. If you can't add to her life, don't even try to arrive.

If Trauma Spoke, You'd Never Sleep Again

I never meant to stay.
I was supposed to be a passing storm,
just a bruise in your memory— but
you wrapped me in silence, called me
normal. I became the wallpaper in a
house built on chaos.

You tucked me into bedtime prayers
like a dirty secret.
You blamed yourself for my voice,
but I was never yours to carry. I
was handed down, just like your
mother's quiet rage and your
father's missing footsteps.

I show up when the room gets too
quiet. When someone looks at you too
kindly, and your gut flinches, 'cause
love don't feel like safety— it feels like
a setup.

I ride shotgun in relationships.
Whisper lies like,
"They'll leave too. They always do." I pull
the strings when you ghost the ones who
actually care.

I live in your hands—
clenched, always ready to
fight or flee.
You call it anxiety.
I call it memory.

You dressed me in "strong." You
wore me like armor.

But baby, I was always a wound.
And you?
You were bleeding through
smiles, thinking healing was
weakness.

But I see you now—
asking questions, holding
your own hand. Making
space for softness
without letting go of grit.

Keep going. Speak me
out loud, drag me
into the light.

I hate that.
It's how I die.

Dear Me, Before the Damage

I saw you the other night in a dream I
didn't want to wake from— barefoot,
holding your pain like a teddy bear no
one told you you could put down.

You were seven, but your eyes were
grown. You already knew how to hide
hunger, how to dodge hands, how to
smile through silence.

I sat next to you on the porch steps.
Said, "Hey... I know you."
You looked up like maybe,
just maybe, you'd finally
been found.

"I tried to be good," you
whispered. "I tried to be
small enough so they'd
love me."

I swallowed a sob and said,
"That wasn't your job."

You thought the yelling meant you failed.
You thought the leaving meant you weren't enough.
But sweet soul, you were never broken.
They were.

You didn't get to be soft, so
I'm learning how now. You
didn't get to cry,
so I do it loud enough for
both of us.

You gave me your survival, I'll give you back your peace. And every time I choose to rest, to say no, to love gently— I'm writing you a new ending.

Still Here, Still Standing

It’s doing the dishes when
your mind is screaming. It’s
getting out of bed on a day
that feels heavier than the
world should allow.

It’s replying to texts you don’t have the energy to
answer just so people don’t worry. It’s laughing in
group chats when you just cried in the bathroom
stall at work.

Survival is invisible.
No finish line.
No audience. Just you,
and your body, and the
decision to stay.

You celebrate in whispers— “I
didn’t cancel the appointment.”
“I ate today.”
“I didn’t answer his call.”
Tiny victories that feel
like war medals you
hang in secret.

Nobody claps for the mother who holds
her breakdown until bedtime. Nobody
sees the man who doesn’t text back the
dealer. No one celebrates the child who
breaks the cycle quietly by not yelling
back.

But I see you.

I know this strength.
It's ugly, it's sacred.
And it's yours.

Still here.
Still fighting.
That's enough

Blurred Lines in Black Skin"

Too Black for comfort, not
Black enough for belonging.
You speak "too white," walk too
soft, think too loud.

You code-switch in your sleep,
apologize for your brilliance, dim
your damn light just to fit rooms
that weren't even built for you.

You wear your hair natural, and
they call it rebellion. You
straighten it, and they say you
lost your roots.

If you read James Baldwin,
you "deep." If you twerk at
brunch, you "ratchet."
Ain't no room to be both.

You grew up on Lauryn Hill and Jay-Z. You
pray like grandma taught you but cuss like
your cousins from up the street. You a
contradiction in gold hoops and trauma.

They say you too ghetto.
Too loud.
Too angry.
But you BEEN quiet—
they just ain't listening.

In the boardroom,
you tuck your slang in your sleeve.
At the cookout, you feel like an

outsider for chasing degrees
instead of dreams they could see.

You wear your ancestors in your walk.
You carry the South in your vowels.
You hold generational pain like
second nature. And STILL, they
ask if you Black enough?

What's Black enough, then?
A felony?
A baby mama?
Trauma tattoos and EBT cards?

You are Black in all shades, from
books to beats, from locs to lace
fronts, from trap houses to
scholarships.

You Black in your joy. Black
in your healing.
Black in your rage.
Black in your softness.

You ain't gotta shrink, ain't gotta
choose. You ain't a stereotype—
you a spectrum. A universe in
melanin, spelled in ebonics and
excellence.

Black ain't a box.
It's a galaxy.
And you?
You the whole damn sky.

"When Strength is a Sentence"

They call you strong
like it's praise, but
it's a trap.
They mean,
"We need you functioning."
"We need you silent."

You hold everyone else's breakdowns like
unpaid rent.
They cry.
You comfort.
You cry?
They vanish.

You wake up tired, go to sleep
exhausted. And somewhere in
the middle, you lie through
your teeth—
"Yeah, I'm good." You
say it so much, you
start to believe it.

No one checks on the strong friend.
No one brings you food, holds your
hand, tells you,
"You don't have to do this alone."

But strength isn't never breaking. It's
choosing to stay alive when
disappearing would feel like peace. It's
saying "help" even if your voice shakes.

You're allowed to collapse.
To scream.
To not hold the world up for once.

Strong don't mean silent.
Strong don't mean alone.

"My Circle in Satin"

In satin and strength, they stood with grace,
Each one a memory I can't replace. Bridesmaids,
but more—they're pieces of me, Bound by love,
history, and loyalty.

Sharkieka, my big sis, my first best friend,
A steady soul on whom I depend. She
wiped my tears before I knew why,
Taught me to rise, to dream, to try. Her
voice, a balm through every storm, Her
love, a shelter deep and warm.

Shawniece and Patty, my double flame,
Two hearts, one rhythm, never tame.
From playground days to grown-up talks,
We found ourselves in midnight walks.
From scraped knees to womanhood's
test, We never let the world steal our rest.
Through every call and every cry, We
held each other, eye to eye.

Carrie, my baby, my little light,
With the softest heart and fiercest fight.
A little sister with the wisdom of years, You've
caught my laughter and caught my tears.
In your presence, I feel at peace, A
kind of love that will never cease.

Then Sarita, my soul I met at sixteen,
Where dreams were tough but hearts were clean.
At Job Corps we found a quiet grace, No
battles—just peace in a shared space. A
sisterhood formed without a fuss, No
blood, but still—it's always us.

And Nawaal, a spirit I didn't expect,
But one whose heart I deeply respect.
We built a bond both soft and strong, A
kind of right that can't be wrong.
With every laugh and silent nod, She's
been my mirror, my friend, my God.

Through every breakdown, every cheer,
These women stood and drew me near.
From little girls with scraped-up pride,
To grown queens walking side by side.
They know the me that's torn and true—
And still said "yes" when I said "I do."

So this is my circle, my sacred crew,
Loyal, wild, and deep like dew. Not just
bridesmaids—they're my song, The
ones who've held me all along.

Forever bonded, come joy or pain,
Through sunshine bright or pouring rain.
Because of them, I walk with pride—
With love that never leaves my side.

www.ingramcontent.com/pod-product-compliance
Lightning Source LLC
LaVergne TN
LVHW090430210926
848480LV00002B/760
* 9 7 9 8 3 4 9 4 4 8 9 4 2 *